D0563341

# LEMONS *to* LEMONADE

### Overcoming Your Past & Winning in the Now!

## CHRISTOPHER L. WALKER

Unless otherwise indicated, all Scripture quotations are taken from the Amplified Version of the bible.

Some quotations are taken from the New Living Translation, New King James, King James, Message, NIV and Amplified Version of the bible.

1st Printing

Lemons to Lemonade© –Overcoming Your Past, Winning in the Now!
ISBN 978-0-615-83138-1

Copyright © 2007 by Christopher Walker International
P.O. Box 120337
Clermont, FL 34712
www.cathedralofpower.org

Published by
Innovative Creative Enterprise (ICE) Media Group
P.O. Box 120337
Clermont, FL 34712

Printed in the United States of America. All rights reserved under International Copyright Law. This book or parts thereof may not be reproduced in any form, stored in a retrieval system, or transmitted in any form by any means- electronic, mechanical, photocopy, recording, or otherwise- without prior written permission of the publisher, except as provided by United States of America copyright law.

Book Cover Design & Interior Layout by:
Fellowship Media
407-434-9680
www.FellowshipMedia.net

# Endorsements

"I love a 'rags to riches' story – a story of ultimate success that starts with picking up after a loss! These stories provide inspiration and awaken confidence. In Lemons to Lemonade, Chris Walker celebrates the champion and also takes a deeper look at the purpose behind the difficult times. Enjoy this book, and be encouraged as you create your own story of success!'

**Dr. Dave Martin - America's #1 Christian Success Coach and Author of Twelve Traits of the Greats**

I believe that all of us can see a portrait of ourselves in this book. Each of us has experienced some difficult lemons at one time or another that seemed impossible to navigate through. Pastor Chris has even taken us on a personal journey of his own defeats and triumphs and the process that we must be willing to endure. I recommend this book to anyone who wants to step out of their past pain and into their divine destiny!

**Dr. Yvonne Capehart - Sister Keeper Intl' Ministries International Speaker and Author**

*'Is it a problem or a promise?'* That's just one of the probing questions addressed in Chris Walker's insightful book, *"Lemons to Lemonade."* With compassion and candor Pastor Chris encourages readers from every walk of life to take their painful and traumatic events and use them to become champions of a

better way. This book is a must read for those struggling in the mire of life's adversities for in it they will find how to turn their struggles into strength."

**Dr. Anya M. Hall - TeKton Ministries Int'l, Speaker, Author**

-As we enter into the greatest decade of mankind, we need a catalyst that will inspire us to create the future in the present. We need a fresh voice instead of an annoying echo that will encourage us to move past our past. We need someone who can teach us to take the lemons of life and squeeze them, until they holla! Pastor Chris Walker has done it and all I can say is let the world say AMEN!

**Dr. Simon T. Bailey - Award-Winning and bestselling Author of "Release Your Brilliance"**

In Chris Walker's latest book, *Lemons to Lemonade: Overcoming your past, Winning in the Now!*, will give you the inner strength to charge to your future. God has prepared for every one of us, a great future that is worth running to everyday. There are circumstances in our past that tries to own us and tell us what we can and cannot do. This must read book will help you let the past be the past, and the future a place you are running to with all joy and expectation.

**Dr. Roberts Liardon - International Speaker/ Author of the bestselling series "God's Generals" Sarasota, Florida**

4

*Like lemons* there are seasons where life squeezes the best out of us. Chris reminds us, there is always a pitcher of purpose that releases the refreshing water of the word and the sweet commune of the Holy Spirit. Pastor Walker has penned his life passion in this must read of "Lemons to Lemonade".

**Pastor Jerry Grines - Kingdom Family Ministries, Lake Mary, Florida**

Pastor Walker's book takes you on a personal walk through the fire. I have lived it with him to some extent and can understand his passage though the -valley of the shadow of death. It moves me to see how he has used this arduous journey to change lives, and to put it into writing as a road map for others to follow. This is indeed a great book to be read, studied and read again.

**Pastor Chris Johnson - House of God, Mt Dora, Florida**

This book is simply amazing and full of wisdom that will help navigate the reader to purpose and destiny.

**Pastor Mark Knowles - Deliverance Tabernacle, Nassau Bahamas**

Pastor Chris has pushed the can do button of so many through his passionate writings in the book Lemons to Lemonade! Anyone who has entertained the idea of quitting on their dreams, visions or destiny will be inspired to abandon the thought and activate their possibilities. Great job Pastor Chris and thank you for pushing the button!

**Apostle Dannie Williams - Citadel of Hope Ministries, Leesburg, Florida**

# Dedications

I dedicate this book to my loving wife, Carla for your inspiration, patience and encouragement of writing this book. Also for the many prayers, endurance and understanding during those lemon seasons. Together we are now making the best lemonade!

To my children Marquis, Justin, Jael, Charles, and Victoria, & Chris Jr, live your dreams and become the greatest and always trust God.

My Grandmother, Eva L. Williams (mama), thanks for bringing me up in the way that I should go because when I got older I didn't depart. And for introducing me to the greatest, Jesus!

My Mother Carolyn H. Lewis thanks for bringing me into this world so I can have a story to share.

My Father & Step-Mother, Kenneth & Ethel Walker, for teaching me to work hard, be determined, and never quit.

Dr. Earl & Beverly Carter for your relentless stand in the Body of Christ and for teaching me to not waddle in my lemons but go after life's lemonade.

Bishop Clint S. Brown and the Faith world family for building my Faith and making my baby jump! You've been the greatest inspiration!

Larry & Renay Pressley for being there for me in my lemon season at a time when I needed you the most. You saw me be squeezed but you knew God had a plan and a presentation for the world!

My Church family, Cathedral of Power Intl the greatest group of people that I could ever Pastor. You guys are awesome!

Apostle Dannie & Dr. Precious Williams, for teaching me how to live a maximized life. Your example of integrity, character, and faith is valuable.

Bishop Ronald Kimble, for your many years of encouragement and your profound wisdom that has helped me in my ministry and my walk with Christ. Your friendship is priceless!

To all my friends who took the time to endorse this book, thanks so much it means a lot.

Dr. Dave Martin. -Force of Favor was the first book I ever read from beginning to end. It changed my way of thinking, now I'm walking in the F.O.G. (Favor of GOD!)

Author Delatorro McNeal, —The Greatness Guy you made me believe that my story was worth sharing and that I could write this book. Thank you!

David and Tammy Lawrence thanks for being a solid friend for over 20 years, and for your continued encouragement.

# Table of Contents

Lemonade Manuscript ©2007

"When life throws you a lemon, make lemonade"

- UNKNOWN

# *Introduction* - **Life is full of lemons**

*In* life every person has had at least one story of suffering or something that they have gone through or are currently going through. We would normally classify these as lemon situations. Lemons are sour and they are bitter, they just don't taste that good. And there are some things that many of us have gone through that are bad memories for us, but God wants you to understand that those lemons can be turned into lemonade.

Many of us would classify these obstacles and pains in our life as lemons; things that looked promising but somehow they went sour and put a bitter taste in our purpose. There are many lemons in life that can be a sour experience for us but we must remain prayerful and faithful to the end until God turns our situation into lemonade.

Now the truth of the matter is life is constantly throwing us lemons. As a teenager I use to listen to old school music because my father was a collector of music. He use to listen to a song called, -If it ain't one thing it's another. In other words something is always bound to take place that we don't like. The key principle here is will you turn it into lemonade, or will you keep receiving the bitter taste of the lemons of life? This is all governed of course by your attitude and perspective of how you see your situation. In other words you will either see what you're going through as a problem or a promise.

I know right now because of the disappointment you may not understand until later that you had to go through what you went through. The old folk use to say everything happens for a reason. So until God reveals what that reason is, go through with your head up high knowing that there is purpose in this pain.

I love lemonade and just the fact that I am mentioning it makes me want to go out and get a glass of it right now. I believe you could eat something all day long and even drink water or another beverage; but if someone offers you a cold glass of lemonade something begins to water in your mouth and you begin imagining how good it will taste. Often the phrase -making lemonade expresses the ability to triumph over adversity. We all get our share of lemons. Be it a vehicle that turns out to be a -lemon or a home that consistently needs repairs like the one in the Ice Cube movie, -Are We Done Yet.

*Learn how to squeeze purpose out of those lemons...*

But in order for the lemonade to become lemonade there has to be some lemons. You won't get the lemonade without some issues, pain, and hurt. Author Delatorro McNeal -the Greatness Guy once said that every book that you read, every CD that you buy, and every story of tragedy to triumph is somebody's lemon that was turned into lemonade. And God wants us to understand that no matter what you have gone through just learn how to squeeze purpose out of those lemons so you can enjoy the lemonade.

There are people reading this book right now and maybe you've gone through some very unbearable situations in your life but you will have to make a decision today to either carry around the basket of life's lemons or the glass of lemonade's purpose. No doubt some of you who are reading this book have experienced enough in your lifetime to write your own book or manuscript to your own movie. I believe that God wants to take your *testimony and turn it into a textamony* so that others can read it and be refreshed, renewed, and refilled. People will pay lots of money to hear about somebody else's lemons or story of hardship that they overcame. We all like a pit to the palace story and find it interesting how people were able to pull themselves out of a challenging time in their life.

We look at people like Oprah Winfrey who had many stories of growing up being abused by relatives and then later on in life battling a weight problem. But even though she went through many years of lemons or hardship she knew inside of her was a lemonade story. She went on to become one of richest women in America and the #1 daytime syndicated talk show host of our time. Oprah also stated her own TV network, THE OWN Network, where she now gives others the opportunity to sell their stories around the world to millions of viewers.

*In Proverbs 4:7 says, "Wisdom is the principle thing; therefore get wisdom and in all your getting, get an understanding".*

So no matter what happens in your life and no matter how catastrophic the circumstance, it is each person's responsibility to turn that experience into lemonade. We constantly see examples of people doing this daily. They do this as a means to heal themselves and create meaning.

There was a woman whose son was killed by a drunk driver, so to prevent this from happening to someone else and so that they didn't have to suffer like she did, she created and organization called MADD (Mothers against drunk driving).

There have been people who have been diagnosed with Aids or Cancer and they decided to give up everything and dedicated their lives traveling the world to raise consciousness about the diseases.

No matter what the situation of life is, learn how to play the hand that you have been dealt. Even people who have made major mistakes in life where the entire world found out about it, like former President Bill Clinton did, can transform that lemon into lemonade by practicing true humbleness and humility.

I have had the awesome opportunity to minister every month for the past four years at a Federal prison and have met some great men and women who just ran into some lemon seasons in their lives.

I always try to encourage them that life isn't over just because you're behind bars. Maybe your reading this book and you're sitting in Federal or State Prison, just look at it as a spiritual retreat rather than focusing on the mistake you made or the time you have left.

Scripture says that wisdom is the principal or most important thing and in all your getting get a full understanding, So as you continue reading this book we are going to get an understanding of the five purposes of lemons in your life and the seven step process that we all must go through in order to walk in our lemonade lifestyle consistently.

"Life isn't about waiting for the storm to pass, it's about learning how to dance in the rain."

- UNKNOWN

# Chapter 1.
## All Lemons Have a Season…

*As* a child growing up, I once heard this song by a young singer named –Little Orphan Annie. She was popular for singing the song entitled, –Tomorrow. The lyrics went as follows:

*The sun'll come out*
*Tomorrow*
*Bet your bottom dollar*
*That tomorrow*
*There'll be sun!*

*Just thinkin' about*
*Tomorrow*
*Clears away the cobwebs,*
*And the sorrow*
*'Til there's none!*

*When I'm stuck with a day*
*That's gray,*
*And lonely,*
*I just stick out my chin*
*And Grin,*
*And Say,*
*Oh*

*The sun'll come out*
*Tomorrow*
*So yagotta hang on*
*'til tomorrow.*

The song simply was saying, even though there may be lemon seasons in your life today, you must not focus on the rain or the clouds, because after the rain there is always sunshine, so hang on until it comes. In the book of Daniel we learn about a young teenager named Daniel who faced many rainy and cloudy times in his life. One day he was taken from Jerusalem into captivity in 605 B.C. And for more than 60 years of his life in Babylon, Daniel faced many lemons, but in all those years, he grew stronger in his commitment to God. From his youth, Daniel was determined to live by God's law in a foreign land. In moments of crisis he turned first to God in prayer; his enemies would later use his regular prayer time to trap him.

The book of Daniel paints a beautiful picture of a young man who lived out his commitment in seasons of experiencing many lemons in his life. In Daniel Chapter 6 we see that King Darius was reorganizing his Kingdom, so he appointed 120 princes (governors) to administer all parts of the Kingdom. He also appointed three vice-regents of whom Daniel was first. These 120 governors were to give account to the vice-regents whose job was to make sure that the Kingdom was in order. But because Daniel operated in excellence and wisdom, he was preferred above all the governors and vice-regents, so the King put him in charge of the entire Kingdom.

Well you can imagine that jealousy begin to set in among the other leaders. So the other vice-regents and governor began to plot his demise or how they could bring him down. But after searching his character they could find no evidence of negligence or misconduct. So they finally gave up and said, "We're never going to find anything against this Daniel unless we can cook up something religious." They knew that the only way to get Daniel in trouble was by catching him doing what he loved to do the most, which was praying to God.

So they wrote a policy that stated that no one could pray to their God and if they were caught they'd be thrown into the Den of Lions to their death. So the King passed the law and signed the decree. Then they set him up and turned him in to the King who really didn't want to do anything to Daniel, but he had signed the decree, which meant death for Daniel. So the King stayed up all night praying and fasting for Daniel, trying to figure out how he could get Daniel out of this situation because he loved him.

Daniel 6: 14- 21 (Message) *14 At this, the king was very upset and tried his best to get Daniel out of the fix he'd put him in. He worked at it the whole day long.*

*15 But then the conspirators were back: "Remember, O king, it's the law of the Medes and Persians that the king's decree can never be changed."*

*16 The king caved in and ordered Daniel brought and thrown into the lions' den. But he said to Daniel, "Your God, to whom you are so loyal, is going to get you out of this."*

*18 The king then went back to his palace. He refused supper. He couldn't sleep. He spent the night fasting.*

*19-20 At daybreak the king got up and hurried to the lions' den. As he approached the den, he called out anxiously, "Daniel, servant of the living God, has your God, whom you serve so loyally, saved you from the lions?"*

*21-22 "O king, live forever!" said Daniel. "My God sent his angel, who closed the mouths of the lions so that they would not hurt me. I've been found innocent before God and also before you, O king.*

## I'm still here!

You must know that even though someone may put you through a lemon situation, God can cause others to work on your behalf and even give you an opportunity to display God's miracle working power. So the next morning the King went to the den and cried out to Daniel, -are you still here, and Daniel said, -Oh King I'm still here! Daniel was able to go through his lemon situation for a season and through the power of God he was able to stand in faith.

I believe because of Daniel's faith he was able to go into his lemon situation with the confidence that God would deliver him. And while he was there God supernaturally gave him dominion over the lions! The people who snitched on Daniel, I believed began to rub their hands in joy thinking that this was the end of him. They were jealous and didn't like the favor that he was getting from the King.

Know that there are people who have been jealous of you for a long time and are waiting on your demise, waiting for you to be taken out by your lemons thinking that the things that they have said to you or even about you will take you out, they have been declaring that you will not make it but they don't understand that this is just for a season, this too shall pass! You've got to be like Daniel and tell the naysayers -I'm still here!

Maybe you're being attacked on your job because you are getting favor from your boss and you haven't been there as long as the others and some can't understand why you are being promoted or favored above everybody else. So they've began to plot against you thinking that they are

20

going to take you out. But if you stand in the midst of your accusers and trust God he will supernaturally bring you out like Daniel, and you can go to work and shout, -I'm still here!

Maybe you've had a difficult financial time in your life and the bank is threatening foreclosure, or you've recently lost your job that you've had for years and don't know how you're going to make it. Perhaps your family and friends have turned their back on you when you needed them the most and you feel all alone. But if you trust God in your lemon hour you'll be able to shout, I'm still here!

## *Keeper of the dream*

Comedian/Actor/Author Steve Harvey no doubt is one of the greatest comedians of our time and known as the King of Comedy of the 21$^{st}$ Century shared his story one day on his syndicated morning radio show. He said that in the beginning of his career life was pretty hard for him. For three years no one knew that he was homeless and that he lived in his car. He could not afford to have a place to live because he only made $275 to $300 a week doing comedy shows. So to keep himself clean he would search out for a Ritz Carlton Hotel because they had bathrooms on the 1$^{st}$ floor, plus he liked the fact that they had fresh hand towels in the restroom. Whenever he needed to bathe himself he would go into the rest room and take a few hand towels and wet them with water and hand soap.

He would then take them into the stall and bathe himself to keep himself clean. One day as he thought about how his life was going, how he had to hide this embarrassing lemon or season in his life, it seemed as though the break in the industry, that he longed for would never come. He began to cry as he felt like he was a failure in life. There he was making people laugh every night while he cried everyday inside. He was at his lemon moment. Then he heard the voice of God tell him, -Son I'm going to take you to places you've never seen before.

Steve Harvey went on to become a multimillionaire having had his own syndicated sitcom TV show for seven years, landing acting roles in several box office movies, hosting national music award shows, being crowned the King of Comedy, and hosting his own daily national syndicated radio show in 60 markets across the country. He also became the new host of FAMILY FEUD game show and landed his own daytime show, THE STEVE HARVEY SHOW on the NBC Network.

Steve is also the winner of several NAACP Image Awards and the winner of the Martin Luther King Jr. -Keeper of the Dream Award. He has currently written two books which within months became #1 on the New York Times Best Sellers list. One of his books, "Think Like A Man" was made into a movie and earned 100 million at the box office in 2012. He is now enjoying & experiencing his lemonade and we are drinking it every time we laugh, listen, and watch his show.

Like Daniel in the Lion's Den, Steve can shout, -I'm still here! Because Steve didn't give up and went through the process of his sour moments, he can now help millions of listeners daily to go through their lemon seasons.

Jan Crouch is Co-founder of the re-known Trinity Broadcasting Network (TBN) which has become the largest television network in the world surpassing the CNN Network. One day Jan encountered her own lemon season. In 2003, Jan was dying of colon cancer. The doctors said without chemotherapy and radiation treatments she would have only six months to a year to live. Trusting that healing was possible, she refused any and ALL of the doctor's advice, except removal of the active tumor, and placed her faith fully in Jesus!

Jan recalls her appointment at the Doctors office seeing the image of the cancerous tumor on the screen. She remembers hearing those piercing words that anyone can hear —-Mrs. Crouch, we have discovered cancer in your large intestine. The Doctors revealed to her that she had C3 colon cancer, cancer of the appendix, spots on lungs and liver, and 3 out of 5 lymph nodes had cancer. Even with massive chemotherapy and radiation she would only have a good 2 years, but without it maybe 2 months.

Jan was determined that this lemon season wasn't going to last long, she settled in her heart that healing was her portion. She said, no to chemotherapy and no to radiation. Jan declared, -I am healed in Jesus' name. And, yes, ten years later she is -Still here living a lemonade lifestyle. She is alive and well, giving her life completely to TBN and telling millions around the world daily about her great miracle from God! Because Jan didn't give up now those that are watching TBN looking for encouragement or facing cancer can find hope and refreshment through her testimony.

Thomas Edison a great inventor of the 19$^{th}$ Century was the inventor of the light bulb and after trying over 10,000 times he finally got it right. Someone asked him how it felt to get it wrong so many times, he replied, -I have never failed I just found 10,000 ways that didn't work.

However long your season lasts, be willing to stick it out until something happens. Know that it won't last forever and while you're waiting make everyday count. I'm glad

Thomas Edison didn't stop during his rough season when things didn't work, because now I don't have to write this book in the dark or write it by hand.

*"The ultimate measure of man is not where he stands in moments of comfort and convenience, but where he stands at times of challenge and controversy."*

- DR. MARTIN LUTHER KING JR.

# Chapter 2.

## Lemons are not meant to hurt you, but to challenge you...

*Daniel* 6:23 *Then the king was exceedingly glad and commanded that Daniel should be taken up out of the den. So Daniel was taken up out of the den, and no hurt of any kind was found on him because he believed in (relied on, adhered to, and trusted in) his God.*

Scripture says that the next day Daniel was taken out of the den and no manner of hurt was found upon him because he believed in his God. Your lemon situation or tragedy was not meant to hurt you but to birth you into the next dimension of faith for your life. God has a divine purpose for your life and He knew that someone needed to hear your story. Sometimes when we are going through the most difficult situations in life we don't realize that God is using our situation to build and train us for the next assignment in life.

Someone once said you never know what kind of tea you have until it hits hot water. The same could be true of for us; you never know what kind of faith you have until you are faced with a lemon. We don't necessarily need faith when everything is going good, but we sure realize how much we have or don't have, when we are faced with a challenge.

*"There is always pro-motion in the commotion"*

In Daniel Chapter three, the 3 Hebrew Boys had favor with the King and eventually were put over the whole kingdom and some people didn't like that. They came against them in the same way they came against Daniel. They were accused of not following the status quo & worshipping the idol god and in the process there was a great commotion over their defiance and they were ordered to be put in the furnace to die.

They could have given up and allowed this co-motion to consume them. But as they stood for what was right God supernaturally had already prepared in advance to save them even before they stepped in the furnace.

To the accusers it looked like a lemon day for the Hebrew Boys, but what they didn't know was that God was already in the furnace making lemonade!

*Daniel 3:26 Then Nebuchadnezzar came near to the mouth of the burning fiery furnace and said, Shadrach, Meshach, and Abednego, you servants of the Most High God, come out and come here. Then Shadrach, Meshach, and Abednego came out from the midst of the fire.*

*27 And the satraps, the deputies, the governors, and the king's counselors gathered around together and saw these men--that the fire had no power upon their bodies, nor was the hair of their head singed; neither were their garments scorched or changed in color or condition, nor had even the smell of smoke clung to them.*

*30 Then the king promoted Shadrach, Meshach, and Abednego in the province of Babylon.*

And when they came out of the fire they came out unhurt and then received a promotion.

Maybe you've had some co-motion in your life and it appeared that what you were facing, would take you out, but as you begin to trust God with all the faith that you have (after you've done all you can do to stand, keep standing). Know that during your sour season God was already making preparations for your promotion. You will not only be taken out of the fire of life but you won't even smell like what you've been through!

We must continue to fight daily for our purpose knowing that life isn't always easy and circumstances aren't always favorable. But we do have the assurance that all things will eventually work out for our good. Civil rights leader Dr. Martin Luther King Jr. once said, -The ultimate measure of a man is not where he stands in moments of comfort and convenience, but where he stands in times of challenge and controversy.

It's easy to hang in there when all is going well, but where will you stand when life seem to get the best of you? Will you give up or stand up and take controversy and challenge by the horns? Will you allow the present lemons to take away the opportunity of the greatest season of lemonade in your life?

Know that what you're experiencing now isn't meant to take you out, even though it feels that way. It's not meant to destroy you or even hurt you, but to challenge you and to build you so when you arrive at your purposed destination you will look back and realize why you had to go through the process.

"When you feel like giving up,
remember why you held on for
so long in the first place."

- UNKNOWN

# Chapter 3.

## Lemons teach us to trust God....

*Job* said it best when he had gone through a difficult season in his life, -Thou He slay me yet will I trust Him. Job was like some of us, he had a good business, good life, and he loved his children and wife, and enjoyed his friends. He was an upright man who reverenced God and for the most part made an effort to stay away from corruption or anything that wasn't morally right.

But like Job, we all have experienced a bad season in our life. One day everything in Job's life came crashing down and he began to experience the lemons of life. Within days he lost his children, his hard earned wealth, and his wife questioned his loyalty to a God that would allow him to suffer and his friends questioned his integrity.

But instead of giving up or giving in to life's lemons, Job said I have to trust God through this lemon season in my life even when I don't understand why I'm going through it, even if my wife and friends don't understand why I'm going through it.

And in the end because of his stance and trust in God he received a double pitcher of lemonade! *We often pray, God if you change my situation then I'll change, but maybe if we change; our situation will change.* Change starts with you, if you want God to change your situation then you will have to change and trust Him even when life doesn't add up in the natural.

Then there was the woman in 2 Kings Chapter 4 who dealt with her own lemon situation. Her husband had died, she was out of food, and the creditors that her husband owed, were demanding payment.

The creditors were coming to get her two sons and use them as slaves to pay their father's debt. So not only did she lose her husband, she was now in jeopardy of losing her sons as well. God sent a prophet to her to teach her how to trust Him. She had already made up her mind that she would just fix her last meal and die but God had prepared a way for her to live by faith. The prophet asked her, What do you have of value in your house? she said, -nothing except a little oil and meal.

Many times we don't feel like we have anything of value in our lives, sometime we need to understand that the little that we have is all God needs to turn our lemons into Lemonade. If you've ever made lemonade you know you only need a little lemon juice to make an entire pitcher. Know that God can do much with a little, Matthew 17:20 (Message) says *"Because you're not yet taking God seriously," said Jesus. "The simple truth is that if you had a mere kernel of faith, a poppy seed, say, you would tell this mountain, 'Move!' and it would move. There is nothing you wouldn't be able to tackle."*

Glory to God! Jesus said that there is nothing that we won't be able to tackle if we just trust him through our lemon seasons. Of course we all remember the 911 tragedy of the fall of the World Trade Center buildings in New York City.

I was a high school teacher at the time and remember sitting in my class room getting a phone call from a friend that told me to turn on the television. As I turned on the

TV, my entire class and I witnessed an airplane charge right into the second tower and then moments later we witnessed the fall of both towers.

It was unbelievable! I couldn't help but think of those people who got up every morning at the same time to go to work. Many that day probably thought it was a normal day. Some had dropped their kids off to school or the daycare, went to their favorite coffee shop and then off to work not knowing that their lives would never be the same.

Like Job, they didn't see the lemon situation coming. Many asked the question why would God let this happen? Like the woman in 2 Kings, some asked why did I have to lose my husband or my child at a time like this. Why do I have to lose my job at a time when I'm the only one working in my family? It's in those times of uncertainty that we must trust God even more until we understand.

We have to become like Job and say, I don't know what is going on or even why I'm going through this, God I cannot trace you, but I have to trust you! Today we can read Job's story and be refreshed knowing that his sour season was only temporary and served as a reminder to us today that all of our trust must be in God who is greater than our circumstances. Well keep reading as we see that the purpose of our trials, is never about us but who will come to us.

*"An individual has not started living until he can rise above the narrow confines of his individualistic concerns to the broader concerns of all humanity."*

- DR. MARTIN LUTHER KING JR.

# Chapter 4.

## My lemons are not about me, but others...

*Over* the years I had to learn that even though I may be wrapped up in my own circumstances and wondering why I was going through, I realized that the lemons in my life were not just about me but more about others that I would come in contact with.

Sometime it's hard for us to comprehend that in everything bad that we have experienced, something good can come out of it. Scripture says that, -all things work for the good.... You may say how can a divorce work for my good, how can losing a job or a child work for my good? I'm glad you asked! God can take your pain and use it to mend somebody else who is going through what you are or have experienced.

One day someone will sit down at your table of testimony and hear your story of how you made it through your lemon situation and how you turned it into lemonade. You will refresh someone's thirst for purpose and because you made it, they will understand that they too can make it. One day someone will read your story, one day someone will hear your song that was birthed from a lemon season in your life.

One of my favorite singers and greatest recording artist in the country is Grammy nominated, Stellar Award Winner, Marvin Sapp from Detroit Michigan. He wrote a song entitled,"Never Would Have Made It". This song has become the anthem for those who have experienced life's lemons, knowing that without the help of God they wouldn't have been able to finish the course. And through their experience they became stronger, wiser, and better, thus making lemonade out of their lemons.

But many people don't know that when Marvin Sapp wrote this song he himself was going through a lemon situation. The words of -Never Would Have Made It transpired when Marvin Sapp was left barren in his personal life. Back to back he experienced the deaths of the three most influential men in his life: his father, his musical mentor, and his spiritual father. The lyrics of the empowering song were spoken to Marvin Sapp prophetically on the spot, the date of his recording, and were truly the only way he could have performed on the night that became a critical turning point for him.

The concert took place a day after burying his father and his spiritual father had passed away just days earlier. He recalled having to go preach while the pain of his father's earthly departure was still fresh. **The Lord said to me**, "**Marvin, there's something you need to understand. Although your father isn't with you physically, I will never leave you nor will I forsake you. I will be with you always even until the end of the earth'. This measure of assurance is what he needed before he could utter a note at the live recording of "Thirsty."** I grabbed the microphone and started singing, "**Never Would Have Made It**," says Sapp.

*God knew the world needed hope through a*

*song*

At the time he was also pastoring a brand new church and felt like that he couldn't go on, he felt empty and He found himself in a lemon situation. He thought to himself, how could God take away three of the most important people in my life? But this season in Marvin's life was not about him it was about all of those who needed a glass of lemonade, all of those who needed to be refreshed, all of those who needed to know that there are times in life that we will have to go through the storm and the fire for others. Since I started writing this book Marvin lost his best friend, his wife Melinda Sapp to cancer which in itself is a difficult season in anybody's life. I'm sure God is getting ready to yet release another song to bring healing to the world through Marvin.

God knew the world needed hope through a song. Today millions around the world including secular R&B radio programs still play Marvin's song daily and many find hope and strength. Marvin's album became his best seller of his career. But who would have thought, his best recording came out of his worst experience!

Jesus was the perfect example, He died on the cross and went through a season of being ridiculed, lied on, betrayed, and stripped for His stance for righteousness. But He understood that this was not about Him, but all of mankind. This is why while many were experiencing a lemon and crying at the cross on Friday, He was taking the Keys from the kingdom of darkness on Saturday, so we could have Lemonade on Sunday!

Christ greatest moment for mankind came out His worst moment on earth.

*There is Glory Just Around the Corner*

*1 Peter 4:12-13 (Message) Friends, when life gets really difficult, don't jump to the conclusion that God isn't on the job. Instead, be glad that you are in the very thick of what Christ experienced. This is a spiritual refining process, with glory just around the corner.*

People don't care as much about what you go through but rather how you came out! The many men and women of our United States military are some of the greatest heroes of our time who all risked or gave their lives so that others could have peace, prosperity, equality, and the American dream.

They understood that no matter how much opposition that they faced or threats on their own lives, that their lemons were not about them but generations that would be changed for decades and centuries. Remember the 3 Hebrew Boys in Daniel Chapter 3, God allowed them to go through that lemon situation not for them but for all of us who would face a personal burning furnace in our life to let us know that no matter how bad it looks God can bring you out and not allow the situation to take you out!

## My Personal Lemons to Lemonade Story

I myself didn't realize that as I was going through the pains of a failing 1st marriage and becoming a homeless single parent of two boys by the age of 22 that 10 years later I'd be using that lemon in my life to bring lemonade to others who would go through the same thing. As a child I was not fully raised by my birth mother and father. My mother had me and my three other brothers and did the best she could with what she had. We moved quite frequently living in projects and trying to eat as best we could.

My father was traveling in the US Air Force most of my childhood and teenage life. My parents never got married and didn't stay together after I was one year old. I ended up being raised by my grandmother who took me to church every chance she got. Although she did a good job of raising me by the time I was 10years old, I began to deal with the rebelliousness of not being raised by my natural parents.

I thought to myself what did I do and why wasn't I with them. At the age of 11 years old after my grandmother had come to the conclusion that she had done all she could do, she sent me to live with my dad and my step mother.

I was still in my rebellion and rejection stage when I moved to Missouri. For four years it was tough still trying to find my identity, feeling bitter like my life was not going good and living in a small country town I didn't want to be in.

By age 16 I moved back to Florida to my mother's for a few months and then back to my grandmother, set my goals on graduating high school and entering the military as my grandfather and father had done. I figured this way I could get away from my past and start a new life, so I thought.

By the age of 18 years old, I graduated from high school and entered into the United States Army. After basic training and school I went back home to stop by my old high school to see my ROTC Instructor. They had asked me to speak to the students about my job and training as a Medical specialist. It is that day I met my first wife who was a student in the class. Before long we began a relationship and continued it long distance while I was overseas stationed in Korea.

By age 19, I had a baby out of wedlock something I thought I'd never do since I was raised in a Christian home. By age of 20 I was married and within 18 months had two sons.

It was a rocky marriage from the start and one that soon would prove unfruitful and painful. Within the first year my marriage began to fall apart as my wife began having affairs and running around with her girlfriends to clubs and drinking. I found myself with yet another lemon in my life. I felt worthless as a person; I was embarrassed and felt like I had wasted my life on a hopeless dream of being happy for once in my life.

I had so many problems in my marriage that it caused me to get in trouble with my military superiors to the point that they gave me a choice, either send your wife home or don't reenlist. Now my career was in jeopardy and I spent so much time keeping this a secret from my family that I couldn't call anyone to get advice of what to do, so I chose to leave the military (my stability) and go back home to Florida. Before I left, I remember attending a church in San Antonio, Texas where I was stationed called New Creation Fellowship with Drs. David and Claudette Copeland.

We had frequently visited this church and always were uplifted by the pastors inspiring messages. One Sunday after church while my wife went to the restroom, I walked up to Dr. Claudette to shake her hand, she took my hand and looked me in the eye and said something I've never forgotten. She said, −God has a plan for your life and a great calling, but He can't fulfill it because you're married to the wrong person.

I was shocked because she didn't know what I was going through but God did. The following week we packed up our stuff and moved back home to Florida. I went from having a steady living, new car, and my own place, to living with my oldest brother and being jobless all while still having a broken marriage.

In the third year of marriage a brick was thrown at me as I discovered that my oldest son was in fact, not my son. I felt like I had lost my life to a bucket of lies and deceit. But I was so embarrassed I couldn't dare tell my family, mother, or grandmother. This was by far the worst lemon in my life, so I thought. Then the un-imaginable happened my wife was pregnant again but this time by someone else.

I thought, here's another lemon that I can't bear. She later decided to have an abortion and not keep the baby and asked for forgiveness. A couple of more years of this would go on; my wife would go out with her old high school friends who were party girls and drinkers. She would come home late at night and when I complained, I would be told that I didn't know how to have fun and would be called a church boy or I would be accused of keeping her from having a life.

All I could think about is all the times my grandmother told me not to get married, but I didn't listen. One day I came home after working the 3$^{rd}$ shift at the local hospital as an ambulance dispatcher, I discovered that she had packed up her things and left me with the kids.
There I was 22 years old with two kids and feeling like the worst person in the world. I asked God, why is this happening to me? I attempted to hide this from my family, but soon realized that my boys were more important than my pride. So I asked my grandmother to help me raise them.

For months my ex-wife would take me through an emotional roller coaster, saying that she needed time to herself and would be coming home. I would be at work at the hospital making major mistakes when dispatching ambulances. One day my boss called me into her office and asked what was wrong with me. She told me that I had been a good employee but she couldn't understand why I was making so many mistakes on the job. You see in my line of work mistakes could cost someone their life.

I couldn't bear to tell her what was going on at home nd almost broke in tears in her office, so I remained quiet so I wouldn't break. I lost my job that day three days before Thanksgiving and things begin to go down from there. I was so mentality messed up that I didn't realize that I wasn't paying my bills for over three months.

One day I got up to take my boys to my grandmother and my car was gone. I thought someone had stolen it being that I was living in a rough part of town, but after calling the police I realized it had been repossessed. That same week I lost $10,000 in a business deal that went bad, a week later my lights were turned off and I received a letter from the apartment office that they were evicting me. It was a few days before Christmas I was depressed and didn't want to live.

As I was sitting in the dark and depressed, I heard a knock on the door. It was a friend of mine who was a local radio jock. He invited me to his new Church; I didn't want to go at first because I didn't want to hear another sermon on how God can bring me out, but I went anyway and my life was forever changed.

I was introduced to Dr. Earl and Beverly Carter and the teachings were refreshing and uplifting. I became the praise and worship leader and each week Lady Beverly would encourage me and tell me to trust God and declare with my mouth the things that I wanted. The church also taught a lot on marriage and relationships. I couldn't help but think that I wished we had sat in this church and heard this teaching before; maybe things would have been different.

Then one evening I got a call, it was my wife. She was in Atlanta, GA. and wanted to talk. She had been in a relationship with a man there who was abusive. At first I was going to hang the phone up because of anger & bitterness, but I listened. She began to apologize as she had always did, and told me how she had realized that she was wrong and wanted to be back home with her family. She said that she was going to church. I asked her what kind of teachings the church had. And she said that they were teaching on marriage and relationships.

Well immediately I thought that this was God and began to declare that God was restoring my marriage. I testified at church and the church cheered in excitement, not knowing that this fairytale would soon become a nightmare. Within two months she moved back home and stayed long enough to get some money and took off again for another man in New York. I was devastated and went into another depression. I ended up staying with a minister friend of mine Larry and his wife, who took me in for a few days to make sure I would be alright.

I would eventually be able to get myself together and move on with my life and focus on raising my boys. Six months had passed by and just as I was thinking of filing for divorce, I got a call from her again with the same old story of apology and wanting to come back home. Well this time I was not going to have it and I wasn't going to forgive her. I figured my boys had been through enough and needed stability in their lives. So I told her no, along with a few other choice words I don't care to repeat.

A few hours later, I got a call from one of her friends asking me to forgive her. But I didn't see it coming. I would soon fall for it again. This friend even used the scriptures against me. She had told me that since I claimed to be a Christian and knew of God's forgiving grace that surely I could be a living example of His love.

She went on to say that everybody makes mistakes and that my wife didn't grow up in church like I did. So I thought about it for a few days and then did something that I would later regret, I forgave her and took her back.

We decided to make things work for the sake of the kids. Five months or so went by and everything seemed to be going okay, so I thought. Just when I thought I had experienced all the lemons I could deal with, I found out that my wife was pregnant again by another man but this time she was keeping the baby. I didn't know that when I forgave her and took her back she was already pregnant.

For the next 9 months I lied to my family and the church to cover the pregnancy up by saying that it was our baby; I couldn't possibly tell my family and friends that my wife was pregnant and I was not the father. Now I'm going to church leading praise and worship trying to bring joy to those who were listening to me and yet I needed some joy of my own. The baby was born and it was a beautiful baby girl, something that I always wanted, but now I had to live a lie and it was killing me on the inside.

Six months later I got the opportunity of my life, I was asked to produce the first gospel music show for Walt Disney's 25<sup>th</sup> Anniversary Celebration in Orlando, Florida.

44

This was an awesome opportunity as thousands from around the world sat in a packed stadium to see a production idea that God had given to me while I was a student in high school. That event made me my first big paycheck and I was excited as any young 22 year old would be. I had set my heart on taking the money and getting us our own car and apartment since we were living with an elderly lady at the time.

That evening something felt strange, even though it was a night to celebrate my accomplishment, something didn't feel right. When I arrived back to the house where we were staying, the elderly lady sat me down. And began to tell me that she had bad news to share with me. She said she had witnessed my wife on several occasions on the phone having long conversations. She also said that some days when my wife got off work she would arrive home two or three hours late.

I didn't want to believe that she would be involved in something again so I confronted her. It turned into a big fight where she accused me of being paranoid and not trusting her. So she ended up calling her girlfriend and packing her things. I asked her when would she be returning and she replied that she needed time to think to herself and she took the baby girl with her.

At this point I was already attached to the little girl and had accepted her as my daughter even though it was a lie. So I made a commitment to take pampers, milk, and a few groceries over to this girlfriend of hers where she was staying, to make sure the baby had what she needed.

One night while I was at home, something in me led me to go over to the apartment where she was staying. When I got there I didn't knock on the door at first, I saw the curtains slightly opened and I decided to peek in. When I looked in I saw my wife, the baby, the baby's father sitting watching television. Everything the elderly lady told me was true and now I knew why she was having the long conversations on the phone, she had reconnected with the father. I was furious and knew who the person was that she was seeing; I also knew who his fiancé was as well. So I contacted his fiancé, informed her of what was going on. We both drove to the apartment to let them both know that we knew about their affair. I knocked on the door and demanded to talk to them.

Her girlfriend, who was also in the house at the time, shouted through the door that she would call the police if I didn't leave. So naturally I left to avoid trouble. That Monday morning while I was in my classroom at the high school where I worked as a teacher, I got a phone call from my Principal who asked me to come to his office. When I arrived he had asked me about what took place that weekend. I couldn't help but think what she might have told him.

He then said to me, -Whatever happened this weekend was pretty serious because the police department is on their way with a warrant for your arrest. I was arrested that day on my job for attempted burglary, and assault and battery.

There I was sitting in jail facing a potential sentence of 10 years for something I never did. I never touched her or even got near her, although at this point I wish I had. All I did was knock r e a l l y hard on the door and said a few choice words.

As I sat in jail I begin to think about all those warning signs that I had gotten, but ignored. I could hear my grandmother tell me over and over again not to get married.

I thought about the military career that I gave up, I thought about the lie I lived for the baby and now I was in jeopardy of losing my job, my boys, and my freedom. This was certainly a day full of lemons.

## God said, "Now You Know How I Feel

I begin to ask God questions: God what is wrong with me? -Why do I keep letting this person come in and out of my life and I know they will lie again and again. Why is it that I love this person no matter what they do to me, I forgive them even though I know they will do it again?

That day I heard the voice of God so clear like I've never heard it before. He said, -Now you know how I feel! -When I love you and others, I forgive you even though I know you will cheat on me with the devil again and again. During all this God allowed me to experience His heart and His compassion for us.

Through that situation I didn't even know I was going through a Hosea experience. In the bible God instructed Hosea to marry a prostitute and through that process he learned about God's true heart and undying love for His people. I eventually was cleared of all charges and they were dropped. I filed for divorce and was awarded full custody of my two boys and raised them for 8 years by myself. It was tough during those eight years and even at one point we ended up homeless in an abandon house for four months with no water, electricity, and barely any food but we made it. I went to work and church every week and no one ever knew that we were homeless. God took care of us.

## *"Sometimes you have to lose to win again"*

At one point in my life I never thought I'd be able to have a good relationship with anyone. 5 years later as I was at a Christian event called the Judah Music Convention in Orlando, Florida.

There God allowed me to meet a wonderful woman of God name Carla Lee from California by way of Chicago, who was also a single parent of two children; a boy and a girl the same age as my two boys. We had a lot in common and both loved the Lord and music. She had been to several countries around the world doing missions work through her church and was on her way to Greece for a year but God had another plan. I knew she was the one for me, so two weeks later I asked her to marry me and the rest as they say is history!

Thirteen months later we got married and every lemon that I had experienced in relationships in the past suddenly became lemonade. This time I knew this was God's will and purpose for my life as everything begin to fall in place.

All of the lemons and bad relationships I had experienced no longer mattered anymore. The wedding was awesome as all of our bride maids and groomsmen were all ministers. We knew that God was putting us together to advance the Kingdom. Within the first year we had a set of twins together a boy and a girl.

In 2003 we birthed a dynamic church called Cathedral of Power International, and since then we have drawn many families and children to our ministry. My lemon experience is now helping a lot of single parents and married couples who are going through what I went through. I now can also help singles from making that same mistake of getting married too early and for the wrong reasons. I now realize that everything that I went through was not about me; it was for all of those who God was preparing me for, those that I would minister to and bring a refreshing to their lives.

Who would have thought that I would have to lose to win again? International R&B recording artist Fantasia Barrino released a song in 2013 called, "LOSE TO WIN." As I heard the song I begin to reflect on life's many twists and turns. Sometimes you have to lose a job to focus on a calling, sometimes you have to lose a bad relationship to get a true friend, sometimes you have to lose a playboy to get a husband.

For the believers in Christ, maybe even like JOSEPH in the bible, *many times in your losing you win again!* Scripture says, Joseph lost his family relationship, his freedom, and his reputation but in the end he won. God allows us to walk through situations in our lives so that we can help others to win again.

Have you ever wondered, why did God allow the disciples who preached the gospel to end up in prison? Paul and Silas just loved serving God. They didn't pray and praise to get out of prison they praised and prayed because it was the natural thing to do, it was one of purpose and not panic. We can't just pray for God to get us out of our lemons but we must praise Him in our lemons. When the prisoners heard Paul and Silas pray and give God praise, everybody met Jesus even the jailers.

Perhaps you feel bound in your circumstances, know that your prison experience is design to help those in prison become free. Paul and Silas prison experience wasn't about what they did, it was about who they were designed and purposed for.

*Philippians 2:4 "Each of you should look not only to your own interests, but also to the interests of others."(NIV).*

Maybe years from now, like me, you'll come to realize that what you went through, all the pain, the loss, the sleepless nights, the struggles and trials were never about you. It was always about someone else.

"Character cannot be developed in ease and quiet. Only through experience of trial and suffering can the soul be strengthened, vision cleared, ambition inspired and success achieved."

- HELEN KELLER
WRITER, LECTURER, 1880 - 1968

# Chapter 5.

# Lemons help to develop our character...

*Ephesians* 2:10 says, -We are his workmanship, a work in progress that is developing daily. Most people don't want to be developed they just want to hurry up and get the lemonade, not understanding that the lemon process is necessary for the lemonade product.

When I was growing up we didn't have a whole lot of money to buy the name brand foods. Sometimes we would buy the generic or thrifty brand because it was cheaper. When it came to buying lemonade we often settled for the .99 cents Lemon Drink which may have had 1% of real lemon juice in it. So the majority of this drink was really citrus acid, artificially flavored water and sugar. From its outer appearance it had the look and form of lemonade but on the inside it denied all of the power! It was also denying the process.

Even though lemons are bitter it is the lemon itself that validates the authenticity of the lemonade. So in other words you may be going through a difficult situation that seems to be unbearable, but if you are going to be validated in the process; if you are going to have authentic lemonade you will have to be willing to be developed by your trials.

David said in Psalms 119:71, -It was good that I was afflicted that I might learn your ways (your proven process and principles of doing things)......It's good that someone talks about you, it's good when someone leaves you, it's good when the enemy comes up against you, it's good when people turn their back on you.! IT'S ALL GOOD! It is during the affliction that we learn His ways.

Too many people want to be more like Jesus but don't want to go through the affliction or persecution that he experienced. Many people want to settle for the lemon drink of life which has no real process, because it doesn't require as much or the pressure process of real lemonade.

Webster's Dictionary describes the definition of process as this: *a natural phenomenon marked by gradual changes that lead toward a particular result or a continuing natural series of actions or operations conducing to an end.*

In life there is a gradual process toward change. Whether we like it or not sometimes the process of change is needed to change us. But if we learn to hold our course it will result in a positive outcome.

Process also produces and reveals the true character in us. Someone once said that you never know what kind of tea you have until you put hot water on it. In other words, what or who do you become when you're under pressure? When you're going through a storm in your life and you don't know why. It would be great if we could breeze through life with no problems, troubles, or trials, but it doesn't work that way.

The most devastating thing you can do to yourself is go through trials and not grow from or develop out of them. There are lessons to be learned in the process of life, and we must allow ourselves to remain the student. Pride and haughtiness keep us from learning from mistakes and growing in God. When we miss the mark, and many times we will, learn how to forgive yourself and move forward.

When it comes to allowing your lemon circumstances to produce character in yourself, you must identify what type of lemon you are dealing with. By this I mean; some lemons are thrown at you that are out of your control. Others are grown in your very own garden. These lemons are the poor judgment calls we make or the willful agreement to sin, bad choices and decisions that we have the power and control to make. These lemons force you to look inward instead of outward. It is all too easy to place blame on others for the bad things that happen to us, we must mature, grow up and be willing to admit when we miss the mark.

Once you realize that you have caused your own dilemma (if this is the case) seek God for his guidance to help you grow and gain wisdom from it. Let each circumstance you face in life help build your character. Many preachers today would save themselves a lot of trouble and scandal if they could only deal with their character and learn from their situations. I'm reminded of a man in the bible name David who learned from his dilemmas.

In 2 Samuel Chapter 11, King David made mistake after mistake. Within a short time frame he fell into sin. At the very root of David's problems, we find a King who wasn't where he belonged. If David had been out in the battlefield, where the King was supposed to be, instead of hanging around the palace looking at naked women, this whole incident would have never happened. Some have suggested that David may have been battling depression, or having a "mid-life crisis." In either event, he wasn't where he belonged - I should point out here that, when viewed through the eyes of modern western civilization, it's all too easy to conclude that Bathsheba shares in David's guilt as a willing participant. But we also must point out in that society's governmental system, the King was the absolute authority. If Bathsheba was summoned to the King's palace, then she came to the palace or risked execution for defying the King.

Bathsheba's bathing was not in a public place, but probably behind the walls of an enclosed courtyard. She had no expectation that she would be seen, since the King was, after all, supposed to be out in the battlefield with her husband. To make a long story short, David uses his power as a King and sent for Bathsheba, laid with her and she conceived a baby in the process. David tried to cover up the sin by having Bathsheba's husband killed in battle.

This displeased God, so the Lord sent a man named Nathan to tell David that what he had done was out of character. David could have killed Nathan for his open rebuke but instead he admitted to his faults. There was none of the blame-shifting "but" phrases that typified Saul, his predecessor to the throne. There was no excuse, no spin, no double-talk or legalese waffling. David saw his situation clearly, and dealt with it boldly. With his admission of guilt, it would have been fully justified if God had carried out the sentence pronounced upon him by his own judgment and struck him dead on the spot. David confessed his sin, and expected to die for it but God forgave him of his character failure and restored him.

David didn't blame others for his mistake, but rather he grew from them and kept a repentive heart toward God. David went on to become one of the greatest men of character in the Kingdom of God until his death.

True character is measured by what you do when no one is looking or maybe they are! You see what you decide to do or not do, whether private or openly your character speaks for you long after your life has ended. In the Old Testament, the bible said that Job was an upright man who stayed away from lawlessness and honored God. In other words he was a man full of Godly character.

Job became the ultimate example of how you can still maintain your character even when all hell breaks loose around you. Friends turn their backs on you, spouse may walk out on you, and you may not even know why you are experiencing all the numerous of lemons at the same time. Job said, -I don't know what is going on, or why I have to deal with this at this stage of my life, but yet will I trust the Lord! Even when life throws you a few lemons you must maintain your character in God.

Character is defined by Webster's dictionary as; moral excellence and firmness, the attributes that make up a person. Simply put Character is who you are and the convictions that you stand for. Scripture says (He won't put more on you than you can bear). For those of us who know the Lord, we have this assurance and his promise, but we must stand firm on the word of God.

If the lemons of life come to you, God promises to get you through it. Sometimes it's good to approach your lemons with a good mindset, that's half the battle. Your lemons can be a promise or a problem; it's all how you decide to look at it. We must take a winning attitude and our confession must be, -I will live and not die and this situation is not unto death, it will not take me out! Learn how to use your lemons as your stepping stones of development.

# Steps to Successful Lemonade

*"If we had no winter, the spring would not be so pleasant."*

- ANNE BRADSTREET, POET

# Chapter 6.
## Lemons You Need Them

*If* you really want real lemonade you will have to have real lemons. This may sound strange but your problems, trials, and circumstances are necessary for your testimony. As we said earlier lemons are those things in life that were bitter, sour, or undesirable. Things that happened to us that we may not want to talk about or haven't gotten over. These are the things that the enemy wants to constantly remind us so that we stay defeated and give up.

Maybe as a child you were molested by a relative and you have been carrying this secret lemon all these years. You have felt worthless and it has caused you to get into many unwanted relationships. You've probably felt like you wanted to die or it's caused you to view the opposite sex in a negative way.

Maybe you are a product of divorce, you thought the marriage would last forever and that you would grow old together, you never imagined that one day you would come home and that person would be packed up and gone. Now you are a single mother or single father with children and you have carried this resentment (lemon) for 5 or 10 years. Your children have even been affected by the divorce and were left feeling like they were the cause of the break up.

Perhaps you prayed for that dream job and worked 10 or 15 years on it, put money away in a 401-K fund. And then one day just a few years shy of your retirement & full benefits, they laid you off and you lost everything that you worked hard for. Now you have to find a job that is paying what you are used to making and also deal with the drawbacks of trying to get hired. Maybe you're a single mother who got pregnant in her teenage years and have felt like you have missed the mark in life or feel like those dreams that you had to finish school is farfetched. You could also be that mother who had a baby early in life and no one knows, but because you felt like you couldn't raise the baby, you gave it up for adoption and now spend your years wondering what happened to the baby and what they may look like.

Or maybe you're that father who has been working hard to take care of his family but no matter how hard you work it is still not enough to meet the needs and you feel like a failure. You could be that person that is dealing with a habit of drinking, smoking, drug abuse, or sex and you are ashamed of it and have carried this lemon around your entire life and just want to be free from its grips.

Perhaps you are a business owner who has maxed out your credit cards and put everything that you have on the line for your new business and it seems like business is slow and you may have to close the doors and lose your investment. Some of you may be that group of people who grew up hearing nothing but negative words being spoken over your life, you were told that you'd never be anything and have held on to those words and can't seem to shake those lemons that have been spoken over you.

You could be that founding pastor of a new church that has been going for a few months or a few years and you feel like you have used all the faith you have to stay afloat. People are not joining as fast as your dreamed they would, tithes and offerings are down and you've fasted and prayed all you can. Perhaps it's been hard to find committed leaders that even breathe the vision like you do. You're asking God how can I see the faith side of this and

encourage these people that you have sent me to, when I
need encouragement myself!

## *Focus on the juice and not the skin*

We have all at one point or another experienced one,
if not all of these lemon situations. Now sometimes the
-negative things that happen in our life are caused from
personal karma. Sometimes they are caused by other people
or life's circumstances. The truth is it doesn't matter why it
happened or where it came from, for if it happened, you
can be assured that you needed that life lesson for some
reason and the proper attitude is to welcome it, accept it
and look at it as a gift.

It is always the enemy's job to convince us that what
we're going through, we will stay in, but we must never
park in the past of bitterness but rather press toward the
victory that comes after the trial. Many times the enemy
wants to take all of your lemons put them on a gold platter
and present them to you as your destiny in life. He wants to
convince you that you don't have hope and that your life
will never amount to anything. But you have to let the devil
know that you are going to take these lemons and turn them
into lemonade!

The good thing about your bad situation is that the
lemons are necessary for the process. So the more lemons
you have the stronger the lemonade! God's Word declares
that he won't put any more on us than we can bear. In
other words He has built us to handle the impossible and
equipped us to soar above life's challenges. So if you're not
dead and you're still breathing you can handle it!

*Someone once said, "If you're catching hell don't hold it, and if you're going through don't stop."*

Just remind yourself daily it's all a part of the process. You may not understand it or even can see it but know it's a part of a greater picture and plan for your life. Too many times we spin our wheels asking God -Why something is happening instead of asking God to show you the purpose of the situation. We have to be like Job and say, -Lord I don't understand it but I trust you.

Bishop Clint Brown, Senior Pastor of Faith World Church in Orlando, Florida and from whom I learned a great deal from, preached a message called, -Problem or Promise it's all how you look at it. You can see your situation as a temporary problem or you can view it as a promise of something greater to come, it's up to you. You see Bishop Brown didn't know that I was homeless when he preached that message. I came to church every Sunday with my two boys and stood before thousands and encouraged hundreds when I opened up service in prayer. I decided that day to see my homelessness as a temporary situation and, focus on the greater rather than the lesser. So don't despise what you're going through but rather focus on the juice and not the skin, the blessing and the potential is always hidden within.

*"A diamond is merely a lump of coal that did well under pressure."*

- UNKNOWN

# Chapter 7.

## You must be willing to be Cut....

*Diamonds* are the most beautiful stones in the world and have been a source of fascination for centuries. They are the hardest, the most imperishable, and the brilliant of all precious stones. The word "diamond" comes from the Greek word *-adamas"*, meaning "unconquerable".

Diamonds in general when they are mined do not look like what you and I see at the jewelry store. Before you and I can admire and appreciate its beautify and brilliance, it must go through a cutting process. Without going through that process we will never fully understand its value.

The same is true with us; you can't have real lemonade unless you cut the lemon first. The cutting process represents the separation season. We don't like this part of the process because usually it forces us to deal with those things that keep our brilliance from being revealed. Often times it hurts and brings us pain that we don't want to experience. Someone once said, -No pain, no gain. The cutting process is the part that makes us deal with the pain that we have been trying to hide on the inside from others. You never know how bad a piece of fruit is until you cut it open.

Sometimes God has to cut some things or people out of your life so you can have a lemonade experience. Many people today are going through lemon issues because they refuse to cut off some relationships that they know are not healthy or beneficial to their life. There are some people whose relationships had the signs that it wasn't beneficial or that it was abusive, but they chose to ignore it and wouldn't cut it off and ended up dead or mentality scarred for life.

You should always do an inventory of the people in your life or cell phone list or email file. I challenge you to go down these lists one by one and fully examine why each person is there. I was taught, always that people were like elevators they are in your life to either take you up to the next level or bring you down. We have to determine whether people are in our life for a reason or a season.

Some people that you were in high school or college with were good for that season of your life. But when God is trying to shift you, some of your relationships won't be able to shift with you. Don't try and hold on to the old memories of the good old days because God is trying to get you to the lemonade. (Jesus asked can you drink of this cup) everybody can't drink from the same cup.

So maybe you need to cut out some friends that you have in your life that are negative. You know the people that when your phone rings and you see their name on the caller ID you begin to dread answering it because you know it will not be a fruitful conversation. Instead of programming their real name in your phone maybe you should try words like (gossiper, hater, trouble, or negative) so when your phone rings and the word negative pops up on your caller ID you know it's just negativity calling with more drama.

For some of you it's not your friends but your own relatives that you may need to cut for a season because they don't understand where you're going or even who God wants you to be. In Genesis we find Abraham is traveling with his nephew Lot.

But there came a season where Abraham had to separate himself from his own nephew and when he did God showed Abraham all of the blessings that he wanted to give him. Sometimes we have to separate ourselves from people so that God can talk to us and show us our purpose and how to fulfill it.

For others that are reading this maybe there are hidden issues in your life that need to be cut out. The bible instructs us to lay aside every weight that so easily gets us off track. Identify what is weighing you down and getting you off track and be willing to cut it. All of us know those things that cloud our focus and the things that constantly hold us back from making progress.

Every minute in life is a precious gift that we cannot afford to waste and we must guard it with all our strength. Like diamonds we all have a purpose and vary in different shapes and styles. We all may not be the same size or come from the same region, but we all must be cut if we are to shine and bring joy to others as he has designed us to do.

In order for things to grow and develop they must be cut or pruned. Farmers understand this process and use it in their day to day functions. Plants and flowers are pruned (cut back) in order that they may grow and increase. It's amazing to me that God uses this process in nature and it parallels our spirit lives. The challenge in the pruning or cutting back process is to see this process as beneficial and not detrimental. When things are removed it's hard to understand that the removal is for our good and necessary for us to grow, partly because this process is painful and difficult to look at. We must maintain the ability to see the end result and trust the process.

When plants or flowers are not pruned they can actually die or become stagnant in growth and not produce to their potential. So it is with us, when we are not pruned or when we do not allow God to remove the things that hinder our growth we run the risk of not maturing to our full potential.

Take for example Gideon in Judges Chapter 7. The Lord intended to give him the victory but he thought having 22,000 soldiers would be better for the battle. God told him that he had too many and only needed 300 men to win. Now the concept of less is better is easy to understand if you're talking about food intake, but when dealing with battles is hard to grasp, because our natural thinking would tell us that the more men I have to fight the better my chances to win. God's ways are not our ways and His thoughts are higher than ours. In the life of faith we must trust not only in God but also His ways though they may be contrary to what we see, hear, or feel. We must abandon our -senses and accept spiritual laws and processes. For the Lord your God knows the plans He has for you and this process of being cut is to set you up for victory and not defeat.

"There are no shortcuts to any place worth going"

- HELEN KELLER

# Chapter 8.

## You must be willing to be squeezed...

*The* lemon that is handed over by life comes in all shapes, sizes, colors and shades. It is never as straight forward and round and plain yellow as a lemon. The lemon of life could be as huge and devastating as lost job, failed marriage, failed relationships, failed parenting, severe and sudden financial loss or as small yet severe as a moment of embarrassment, cancellation of an important appointment, lack of education, missed opportunity, unexpected delay of flight or just being stuck in a traffic jam! And the worst thing is that there is no invention that can help you squeeze the juice out of such lemon.

The squeezing step is the most important because you have to squeeze out the seeds of bad thinking, sin, procrastination, gossip, lust, hate, and old relationships that you still have, and they've been unable to allow you to connect to better ones. The spirit of fear has to be squeezed out of our life that keeps us from moving forward. Maybe you've desired for a while to start that business but the spirit of fear has kept you from taking the first step because you are focusing more on the fact that you don't have the money, so you continue working on a job where you are not happy. You have been longing for that lemonade relationship but you can't have it because you refuse to squeeze out the seeds and memories of the last two failed relationships that were bad.

Maybe you didn't graduate from high school for whatever reason, and now 20 years later you decide that you want to get your diploma but because of your age fear has told you that it's not worth it. Fear at one point or another has caused many to doubt the power of God.

I'm reminded of a story in the Matthew Chapter 14 when Jesus had sent the disciples to go before him to the other side in a boat while he went to pray. Jesus wanted to deal with and squeeze out their fears. So after Jesus had prayed for several hours it was about 3am in the morning and the disciples were in the boat about 2 miles off shore. The waves and wind begin to get bad and they started getting nervous.

Then as they saw a figure walking toward them on the water and they cried out for fear and thought it was a ghost. But Jesus spoke to them and said be not afraid it's Me. Peter said Lord if it is really You command me to come to you.

*28 Peter, suddenly bold, said, "Master, if it's really you, call me to come to you on the water." 29-30He said, "Come ahead."Jumping out of the boat, Peter walked on the water to Jesus. But when he looked down at the waves churning beneath his feet, he lost his nerve and started to sink. He cried, "Master, save me!" 31Jesus didn't hesitate. He reached down and grabbed his hand. Then he said, "Faint-heart, what got into you?" (Matthew 14:28-31 Message)*

Jesus wanted to know what had gotten into Peter that would cause him not to be able to walk on the impossible, when in fact he was created to do the impossible through his own faith. Peter needed to learn how to squeeze out doubt and fear. If we could all learn how to squeeze out the fears of life then we can get closer to walking in our purpose. It is during the squeezing process that we produce the juice that is needed for the lemonade.

After a lemon has been cut you can see the fruit but if you don't squeeze it you'll never get what is on the inside. You never usually see the real strength of a person until they have been cut by life's circumstances, or are going through a difficult situation. After squeezing five or six lemons it may not seem like you have much because usually there is not a lot of juice. But God can take little things and make them into great things.

Our lives are purposely designed to help others that we come in contact with. And when the people that God has intended for you to touch come into your life, after being squeezed by life's experiences, you will be able to encourage them in their season of despair. And then after you've touched them the cycle begins again as God uses their life to touch someone else that they come in contact with.

You may be asking yourself, " What is the benefit of being squeezed?" Just hearing the word squeezed means that some sort of pressure will come upon you and make you feel uncomfortable. But the benefit of being -squeezed by God is to give us a greater capacity. Webster Dictionary defines capacity as; *the potential or suitability for holding, storing, or accommodating: the facility or power to produce, perform, or deploy.*

In other words, it is our ability to contain or produce. Often our natural or carnal mind tells us that if we are squeezed we are being made smaller, but spiritually speaking you are actually being made larger. For example consider a garbage bag full of paper. Now if I want to get more paper in the bag, I'm going to compress the paper that's already in there so I can get more paper in. The goal is for that garbage bag to carry its maximum capacity. We are squeezed to make room for more! We are squeezed so we can function at our greatest capacity. Pressed down, shaken together and running over!

We must trust that all things will work together for our good. Our daily confession should be –I'm stronger, wiser, and greater than before. When making lemonade the lemon has to be squeezed because what is on the inside is what is needed to produce the end result. No matter how much pressure you feel or how much pressure is applied, the best of you only comes out during the squeezing process. So if you really want the end result of the best of your life, you must be willing to be squeezed.

*"Man cannot live on bread alone, but by every word that proceeds out of the mouth of God."*

- MATTHEW 4:4

# Chapter 9.
## You must add sugar: the Word...

*Man* needs more than just food and water. We need more than Mom's pot roast, vegetables and homemade cakes. Man was designed to be more than just body and soul; he was designed to be body, soul and spirit. We cannot live by bread alone; we need and require every word that proceeds from the mouth of God. The emphasis is on the Words that came from God, not men's words, not what men think about the Word. We cannot live on physical food alone; we need the Word of God. Our bodies are sustained because of the foods we eat, but what about our souls, who we are? We need the Word to feed our minds and our souls so that we may "prosper and be in health, even as our soul prospers" (II John 2).

The Word feeds our spirit so that we can renew our minds to the words that proceed out of the mouth of God and live abundantly like He has intended His people to do. The Word of God gives us the foundation on which to build our lives so that we can live the more-than-abundant life physically and spiritually. God has given us everything we need.

Scripture says that, –Man cannot live on bread alone but by every word that proceeds out of the mouth of God. So having the word in your life is Key to your process. Sugar in this chapter represents the Word of God. The more word you have the better the lemonade. In Joshua 1:8, a young man named Joshua who was Moses assistant had been given the opportunity after Moses death, to lead the children of Israel. God reminded him that as long as he had the word he would be successful.

The more we study God's Word, the more we will be able to gain the wisdom that we need for our process. Scripture says that wisdom is the principle thing and in all your getting, get a full understanding. To bring a full understanding to the sugar or -Word additive to our lemonade we must see the purpose of adding sugar. Sugar is added to sweeten the drink so that it will have a pleasant taste to those who will drink it.

Now, you can have lemonade without sugar and accept the bitter taste. Not adding sugar to lemonade doesn't change the fact that it is still lemonade, it just changes the way it tastes. This is the choice we must make in our situations and circumstances. How much sugar should we add to our dilemma? We have all been given purpose and our lives should be sweeter or better because of the added sugar- Word of God.

Although there are many substitutes for pure cane sugar, there is only one pure cane sugar. For example alcohol and drugs are artificial sweeteners that may give a false sense of happiness in the beginning but in the end bitterness will surface. How many times have we tried to sweeten our lives with things other than the Word of God only to end up empty and unfulfilled? We must fight and resist the temptation of using these artificial sweeteners in our lives.

Simply put, if we want a sweetener that is more fulfilling, we must add the Word and continue to add it to our life on a daily basis. The more Word you listen to the more satisfied you will be. People who are truly living by the Word of God are much happier people. Even when unpleasant and unforeseen -lemon -situations happens, those full of the Word usually respond better. The Word is a buffer against stress, anxiety, worry, anger, and resistance. Scripture declares -He wouldn't put more on you than you can bear. So if you are facing some lemons in your life know that there is a Word from the master to help you bear it. We must be doers of the Word and not just hearers. If we only hear the Word and not live by the Word the end result will be bitterness and lack of contentment. We are spirit beings and our spirits can only be fed with spiritual food.

The most important thing that could have happened to me was when I truly received the Word of God in my life. It no longer became just a book of stories, but a book about people who were just like me or had experienced some of the same defeats, struggles, triumphs, and victories as I had. It was about a God who was so concerned about me that He made sure I had something to read that would identify with every area of my life. It was about a Savior who came that I might have the abundant life.

Scripture says, -Faith comes by hearing, hearing by the Word of God. So the more I expose my mind to it, the more my faith will grow. The more I place myself in a position where my mind and heart are being fed the Word then change will began to take place. I am convinced you can't stay the same after hearing the truth of God's Word.

" He who believes in Me [who cleaves to and trusts in and relies on Me] as the Scripture has said, from his innermost being shall flow [continuously] springs and rivers of living water"

- JOHN 7:38

# Chapter 10.
## You must add Water

*Water* represents God's ability to multiply you in your situation. One of the biggest ingredients in lemonade is water. Water is used to bring all the ingredients together and create an abundance of the drink. Water is the integral fabric in the quilt of life without it, food security, human health, energy supplies and industrial production would be unobtainable. Water is crucial to your health. It makes up, on average, 70 percent of your body weight. Every organ and facet of your body depends on water.

Lack of water can lead to dehydration, a condition that occurs when you don't have enough water in your body to carry on normal functions. Our blood contains 83% of water, muscles are 75%, the brain is 74% and bones are 22% water. So water is very important to our livelihood and health.

Water was scarce in Jesus' day, yet water was as much a necessity for life then as it is today. Just as the physical body needs water to continue living, so does the spirit. Jesus is the water needed by the spiritual part of man. Without Him the soul will eventually die. The soul is thirsty and we try to quench that thirst with many things that satisfy for awhile, but eventually we get thirsty again. The only thing that can truly quench the thirst of the spirit is the living water, Jesus Christ.

We see this demonstrated in John Chapter 4 as Jesus meets a Samaria woman at a well. First, Jesus comes to a town where everyone is a member of a heretical sect. As He sits down by a well, a woman comes to draw water.

Israelites usually don't talk to Samaritans, much less drink out of their ritually impure vessels. But Jesus recognizes her existence and affirms her by being willing to accept a drink from her. Once she gets over her shock, a dialogue ensues. It starts out about water, wells, Jews and Samaritans, but Jesus asks her questions that throw her off a bit and make her think. He finally asks a question that leads her to -tell the truth and admit her need. She's hungry for love, and has run through quite a few partners looking for the real thing. Jesus' soul-piercing glance tells her that His is the love she's been looking for. She abandons her water jar and returns to town to tell everyone about Jesus.

The story shows that Jesus offers divine mercy in the living water of grace, which washes away sins and cleanses souls. The woman went to the well to get a jug of water. Instead, she got much more, including a cleansed and refreshed spiritual life. Jesus is the only thing that can quench the thirst of the spirit.

Anything or anyone else will only wear out and leave the spirit thirsty again. Therefore, Jesus is what my spirit needs in order for me to be able to live eternally with Him. Without the Living Water my spiritual body will die just as my physical body would if I didn't drink any water or other liquids. I will quench my spiritual thirst with Jesus, the Living Water, by looking to Him each day. I will also share the Living Water with others by telling them about Jesus and how He can quench their spiritual thirst like He does mine.

84

If we are to turn our lemons into lemonade we must include God in our process. For the Jesus declares in John 10:10 -I come that you might have life; that life more abundantly. He is saying that once I get in your situation I'll bring everything together, then purpose will begin to take shape.

Water is a substance that can either be contained or released. As we talk about turning your lemons into lemonade, the concept is that the horrible things that happen to us can be turned into opportunities of telling others how God helped us to overcome. The water of God is pure, holy and without reproach.

The water of God is clean so victory then becomes sweet. If I were to make a glass of lemonade with sewer water, it would be horrible to the taste, sight and smell. Serving a pure and holy God makes all the difference and choosing to allow His power to work in our circumstances makes all the difference.

If you are in a dry situation, look for the water. You know, when we truly trust God even though our trials may seem great and full of fire, we can have the testimony of the three Hebrew boys who emerged from the flames without even smelling like smoke. God is able to take what the devil meant to harm and destroy you with and turn it around for your good. There is simply nobody like our God. His power is eternal and there is none greater.

Having God on our side means all things are possible. The Word of God tells us that with man it is not possible, but with God all things are possible. This promise gives us hope that we can come out of any situation. As the Word of God refreshes us then we can turn around and refresh someone else by sharing our hope, trials and triumphs.

The water of God is a great supply of peace and as we walk day by day we must continue to remind ourselves that we have a Savior who was touched with all our infirmities. He understands pain, setbacks and disappointments.

So, He has made a way for us to be victorious in all that we go through if we just simply trust His ways and methods.

"Sometimes your medicine bottle has on it, 'Shake well before using.' That is what God has to do with some of His people. He has to shake them well before they are ever usable."

- VANCE HAVNER

# Chapter 11.
## Shake it Up!...

*One* of the greatest authors and faith teachers of our time on the subject of the Kingdom is Dr. Miles Monroe, the founder of Bahamas Faith International. He says hidden within all of us, we have one of the most powerful tools unknown to mankind, one that has the power to change the course of history.

What is it? It is your God-given gift!

All of us have a gift and our gift is the #1 commodity that we possess outside of our Faith. But we have the responsibility to stir it up ourselves. The apostle Paul wrote to Timothy, *"For this reason I remind you to fan into the flame the gift of God, which is in you" (2 Timothy 1:6)*. The Gift is already there, you just have to learn how to stir it up with a consistent confession of faith! The best person that can stir up that gift is you! You can't expect anyone else to do it for you. King David said it best if no one will encourage you, you got to encourage yourself. How do you do that? You do it by working on or developing your gifts and talents. This is where education and training become important.

Education alone can't hand you your gift, but it can help you develop it so that it can be used to its full potential. Proverbs 17:8 says, "A gift is as a precious stone in the eyes of him that hath it: whithersoever it turneth, it prospereth" (KJV).

In other words, a gift is like a precious stone to the one who has it, once he realizes its value and uses it, it turns into prosperity. If you use your gift, it will take you to your divine destination. Sometime people spend their entire life trying to be like someone else. They imitate their favorite singer, movie star, preacher, or athlete. But God has designed us as originals and has not called us to be like anyone else. You have to recognize what is on the inside of you and be willing to go through the process of squeezing it out.

## *There is something inside of me!*

I love the story about Jazz recording artist, Louis Armstrong. As a kid Louis had always desired to attend music school so he applied and was brought in for an audition. They gave him scales to sing, but he could sing only the first two notes properly, so they told him he didn't have what it took to be a musician. Little did they know he would become one of the greatest that ever lived.

Louis cried because they rejected him from the music program. But Louis told his friends afterward, "I know there's music in me, and they can't keep it out." He eventually became one of the most successful and beloved jazz musicians. He sold more records and made more money than scores of others who were more talented at singing. Now he is forever etched in the history of music.

Even in your lemon season you have to be like Louis and declare –There is music in me and the world can't keep it out! Although we are all born as originals, most of us become imitators. Dr. Miles Munroe once said that he used to think about becoming like everyone else and join the rat race. However, then he realized that if all the rats are in a race, and they win, they simply become the Big Rat. And of

90

course we eventually learn that it's the second rat that gets the cheese; the first rat gets the trap.

Know that you were not created to run in the rat race. Your assignment on earth has been uniquely planned out by God for a divine purpose and if you can just hold on during your lemon season you will find out what purpose is. Scripture says in the book of Jeremiah that before you were born God knew you and had already planned and ordered your steps. Stop asking the question, -Lord why me? and just began to speak like Job, Lord I don't know why this lemon season is here but I'LL TRUST YOU!

Satan is seeking to rob us of our desire to "shake up" the gift of God. But when we become so desperately in earnest about stirring this gift that we are willing to "go the second mile" for the good of others, and that we are willing to bear any burden or make any sacrifice, our joy and peace will be restored by "the God that answers by fire." Stirring in itself is a process that you must be willing to do. It is the stirring that combines the lemon juice, sugar, and water together to produce the end result. Without the process of stirring you just have three elements sitting in a pitcher with the ability or potential to become something refreshing. In all of us is the ability and potential to become something great and refreshing but we must be willing to stir up that potential so that others can be touched by it.

Many years ago, the ability to build a fire was a skill that was vital to many people's survival. Today, most of us simply adjust a thermostat when we want to heat our homes and a gas or electric furnace quickly brings the temperature to a comfortable level.

When many people grew up in South in the 1920's, heating the house was not that easy. Fires in heating and cooking stoves had to be built almost every day. Chopping wood and keeping the wood box full were regular chores.

Through time, they would gain more experience in building fires, they learned that starting a fire was much easier if they kept a live coal from the previous day's fire. To make a fire last during the night and provide live coals in the morning, they would "bank" it at night. Then the next morning, by blowing on or stirring up the coals to get more oxygen to them and make them red hot, they could easily rekindle the flames.

Over 2,000 years ago, the apostle Paul, a highly educated former member of the Sanhedrin, used this simple fire-building analogy to remind Timothy of the marvelous power of God's Holy Spirit. In 2 Timothy 1:6 he wrote, "Therefore I remind you to stir up the gift of God which is in you through the laying on of my hands."

The Greek word for stir, *anazopureo,* "denotes 'to kindle afresh' or 'keep in full flame', It is used metaphorically in 2 Timothy 1:6, where 'the gift of God' is regarded as a fire capable of dying out through neglect.

You cannot neglect the flame that the spirit of God has placed upon you to share with others. Someone needs our flames to continue to burn bright so they can see their way out of their lemon season. As we continue to read God's word we will fuel our flames more and more.

Scripture says, –Oh, brethren, *"Did not our hearts burn within us, while he talked with us by the way, and while he opened to us the Scriptures?"* Yes, indeed they did, and they will start burning again when you Stir Up! Shake it Up! The Gift of God that is already in you!

"I know the plans I have for you
says the Lord, plans to prosper
you and not to harm you, plans
to give you hope and a future."

- JEREMIAH 29:11

# Chapter 12.

## The Ultimate Plan: the presentation

*After* you have gone through the process of being cut, squeezed, and stirred, now God can take your life with all of its past ups and downs, triumphs and victories and present your body and life as a living sacrifice to bring a refreshing to someone else who may be experiencing a lemon season in their life.

Now when someone sits in front of your table of testimony and hears what you have been through, and what God has brought you out of. You will be able to pull out your glass of purpose and pour into them hope, life, and peace. They can look at your life and say if you made it, so can they.

*Good is what God had in mind when he created and designed you and God has not changed what He thinks about you.*

God etched the desire for good things into your heart at birth. That's why it's normal for you to feel frustrated when things are not going well. You sense that something is not as it should be--which is also, by the way, one definition of evil. Evil, from the Greek word "kakos" means *"not such as it ought to be."*

Regardless of our gender, race or nationality, there are some things we all feel we ought to have. We all want to be happy, loved, and find our purpose in life.

I am reminded of a story of a man who found his purpose even after a tragic accident turned his life into a sour situation.

Scott Rigsby was 18 years old when he un-expectantly was hit by a passing 18- wheeler truck, throwing him underneath a 3-ton attached trailer and dragging him over 300 feet. His back suffered third degree burns, his right leg was severed off and his left leg hung barely intact. Scott was hit with a big obstacle as his life was seemingly over and he faced the biggest lemon of his life. Over a decade of countless doctor visits and hospitals, 26 surgeries, additional amputation, depression, fear, and uncertainty, Rigsby had become a professional patient. An inevitable battle with prescription drug addiction followed, as did the loss of many relationships and trust. At one point, things got so desperate that Rigsby sold what little furniture he had just to pay rent. There was no steady income and no dreams for a stable or successful future. The lemons of life had hit Scott Rigsby hard, knocking him down and keeping him there. Scott Rigsby eventually turned his life around, reaching unprecedented heights as a world-class athlete. But it required an unshakeable determination to overcome all of his sour circumstances. Scott Rigsby had to decide that he was going to make lemonade out of his lemons and quickly embraced the motto, -unthinkable, and saw no finish line.

### *There is no finish line*

So in 2005 he decided to change his life, and the world, by breaking down barriers for physically challenged athletes. Little did Rigsby know that his inspirational journey would soon impact generations of able bodied people. Over the next few years Scott would complete in 13 triathlons and 5 road races on his way to setting world records for a double below-the-knee amputee in the Full

Marathon, Half Ironman, and International Distance Triathlon, earning him a spot on the 2006 USA Triathlon Team. On October 13, 2007, after enduring the elements for 16 hours and 43 minutes, Scott Rigsby became the first double-amputee on prosthetics in the world to finish an Ironman distance triathlon with prosthetics at the 140.6-mile World Championship in Kailua-Kona, Hawaii.

His triumphs and adversities during the ordeal is a poetic summary of his life, as he describes the intimate thoughts and feelings of conquering the challenge that ultimately defines his life and purpose. Scott Rigsby's incredible story contains as many highs and lows as one can imagine over such a short and storied life.

Like a Rubik's Cube, there are many twists and turns in his amazing tale that offer something personal and meaningful to each individual. You might laugh and you might cry or, both. One thing is for certain, you will be inspired. Because for Scott Rigsby, there is no finish line.

Rigsby's unique story of success and failures, all started with a decision and the desire to never quit, no matter what, no matter how long. Scott learned how to turn his lemons into lemonade so that we can now be refreshed by his attitude to never quit. Little did Scott Rigsby know that God had a plan and an expected end, to help inspire the world with his life but God didn't use him until he had been broken (www.scottrigsby.com).

Little do we know that as we go through our process someone else is waiting for that glass of lemonade to be set in front of them so they can go on another day. Know that God has great and wonderful plans for your life to be used for the Glory of the Kingdom of God. In His own desire to see them be fulfilled He said He would -never leave us nor forsake us.

Even your life with all of its ups and downs, trials and tribulations, victories or defeats; God can still take all of your lemons and turn them into lemonade if you are willing to present yourself as a living sacrifice unto Him, a demonstration of His will, and transformed for His purpose.

I've always wondered when people made lemonade why would they add a slice of lemon on the edge of the glass. You would think the lemonade was good enough to enjoy by itself. I believe after we've gone through our process of being cut, squeezed, adding the word, letting God in our life and stirring our gift, God adds a slice of our past so that when people sit in front of us we never forget where he brought us from.

So when someone comes to you and say, -I'm going through a difficult time in my life, -you can say -I know I've been there before. Then you can pull out your glass of process and pour them a glass of purpose.

Now close this book and go make some Lemonade! And hey don't forget to shake up and stir up the gift!

# Invitation

*Let* Me Introduce to You My Friend Jesus.

Perhaps you are reading this and it has really been a blessing to your life but you've never come to know the Lord Jesus Christ or have invited Him into your heart. I want to help you by having you say this simple prayer.

-Lord Jesus I come to you with all my lemons in need of a Savior. I give you my heart, I give you my mind, and I give you my soul and my body. This day I declare and degree to the world that I no longer belong to the kingdom of darkness but I now belong to the Kingdom of GOD!

Because of His Word I am a King's kid, therefore I am entitled to the King's benefits in Jesus Name. AMEN!

Welcome to the family of the Kingdom of God!

# 30 Days: Words of Inspiration

_Life Quotes & Personal Declarations'

*Day 1:*      Life doesn't always come with a guarantee but it always come with a price. - **Chris Walker**

*Day 2:*      Sometimes life gets the best out of you and other times you get the best out of life. - **Chris Walker**

*Day 3:*      You can decide today that life is over or life is just beginning! - **Chris Walker**

*Day 4:*      Those who dare to dream are ready to pay the price to make them come true. - **Chris Walker**

*Day 5:*      In our paths are triumph and defeat. Which will you choose? - **Chris Walker**

*Day 6:*      Tomorrow is the greatest day of FAVOR for your life. Wait for it! - **Chris Walker**

*Day 7:*      YOU CAN'T QUIT NOW...YOU'VE COME TOO CLOSE! Keep Striving, Keep Believing, Keep moving forward. Destination: Purpose is ahead! - **Chris Walker**

*Day 8:*      –The way I see it, if you want the rainbow, you gotta put up with the rain.‖ - **Dolly Parton, Country Singer**

*Day 9:*      The purpose of life is a life of purpose - **Robert Byrne**

*Day 10:*    Where there is no struggle, there is no strength.- **Oprah Winfrey**

*Day 11:*    A bend in the road is not the end of the road... unless you fail to make the turn. **" - Unknown**

*Day 12:*    Never allow someone to be your priority while you're just their option - **Unknown**

Day 13:    Death is not the most tragic loss in life. The most tragic loss is what dies inside while you're still alive. - **Dunno**

*Day 14:*    Check your baggage in the past, book your flight in the present, and travel boldly into your future. - **Delatorro McNeal-author**

*Day 15:*    "Perseverance is a great element of success. If you knock long enough and loud enough at the gate, you are sure to wake up somebody.‖ - **Henry Wadsworth Longfellow**

*Day 16:*    Even Skyscrapers are built a brick at a time. The secret to champions is their refusal to quit trying. - **Dr. Mike Murdock**

*Day 17:*    Our greatest weakness lies in giving up. The most certain way to succeed is always to try just one more time. - **Unknown**

*Day 18:*    Many of life's failures are people who did not realize how close they were to success when they gave up. - **Unknown**

*Day 19:*      There are 7 days in a week, and someday isn't one of them. - **Dr. Shaquille O'Neal Former NBA Athlete**

*Day 20:*      If you always focus on what's behind you, you'll never be able to see what lies ahead for you. Change your direction! - **Unknown**

*Day 21:*      Don't look at what might have been, should have been, or could have been! LOOK AT WHAT IS STILL TO BE! God has more for you! - **Unknown**

*Day 22:*      Stay strong; make them wonder how you're still smiling. - **Unknown**

*Day 23:*      Life always offers you a second chance. It's called tomorrow. - **Unknown**

*Day 24:*      Success is liking yourself, liking what you do, and liking how you do it. - **Maya Angelou, Poet**

*Day 25:*      If you cannot do great things, do small things in a great way. - **Napoleon Hill**

*Day 26:*      Don't go through life, grow through life. - **Eric Butterworth**

*Day 27:*      Life consists not in holding good cards but in playing those you hold well. - **Josh Billings**

*Day 28:*    A life is not important except in the impact it has on other lives. - **Jackie Robinson MLB Hall of Fame**

*Day 29:*    My life is my message. - **Mahatma Gandhi**

*Day 30:*    If you live long enough, you'll make mistakes. But if you learn from them, you'll be a better person. It's how you handle adversity, not how it affects you. The main thing is never quit, never quit, never quit. - **William J. Clinton, Former President of the USA**

# Experience the Life-Changing Teaching of Pastor Chris Walker

KNOWN FOR HIS POWERFUL AND DYNAMIC VOCAL ABILITY AS A WORSHIP LEADER, PASTOR CHRISTOPHER HAS THE ABILITY TO USHER IN THE PRESENCE OF GOD WITH BOLDNESS AND FERVOR. HIS PREACHING IS HUMOROUS, DIRECT, PERSONAL AND CUTS TO THE CORE OF REAL ISSUES. HE HAS AN ANOINTING TO BRING HEALING TO THE SOUL AND ENCOURAGE YOU TO REACH YOUR DESTINY. PASTOR CHRIS HAS MINISTERED ACROSS THE COUNTRY AS WELL AS ABROAD IN SOUTH KOREA AND THE BAHAMAS. HIS VOCAL GIFT AS GIVEN HIM A PLATFORM ON CHRISTIAN RADIO AND TELEVISION NETWORKS.

TO SCHEDULE PASTOR CHRIS AT YOUR CHURCH CONFERENCE, OR SPECIAL EVENT CALL 352-321-2930 OR VISIT ONLINE AT WWW.CATHEDRALOFPOWER.ORG WWW.CHRISLWALKER.COM OR WRITE US AT: P.O. BOX 120337 CLERMONT, FL 34712

*Pastor Chris Walker*

# JOIN ME ON THESE SOCIAL NETWORKS

 /ChrisLWalkerSr

 @PsChrisWalker

 Cathedral Of Power
Pastor Chris Walker & Voices Of Power

 /ChrisLWalkerSr

41846255R00061

Made in the USA
Charleston, SC
09 May 2015